WILDERISM DOCTRINE

by

chris wilder

Published by

half book

Fourth Edition November, 2022

The views and opinions contained in this book are not those of the publisher. This book was published in the spirit of free thought, that people may continue to think, grow, discuss ideas, and share the deep thoughts that form our inner beliefs. We encourage you to exercise free will, accept whatever truth you choose to believe, but above all, think and understand.

For more information on Wilderism and the author, please visit www.metashifting.com

Manufactured in the United States of America

Wilderism Doctrine
version 4.01.01 November 04, 2022
Philosophy
Metaphysics

ISBN   978-1-58884-032-5 (print)
        978-1-58884-033-2   (eBook)

TENETS

REALITY IS
SUSTAINABLE ECSTASY
MINIMIZE KARMA
NO MAGIC
EXPAND
CONSCIOUSNESS

INTRODUCTION

Before we get into the tenets, let me explain why I named this belief-system "Wilderism". It's not because I have a big ego and my name is Chris Wilder. It is because I was searching around for a name which would express my intention of creating something which would help get us back to being in tune with nature, with the planet. I think this kind of belief-system is necessary for the survival of our civilization. I am sure that Earth will survive, not so sure about our civilization, meaning the cooperation of great numbers of people. The name "Wilder" comes from the old English, meaning someone who lives in the woods. So even though I will be accused of gross egotism, I still thought it was fortuitous that I have that last name and could use it in this way.

Other Religions

I was raised to respect other peoples' religions, at least to their faces. People can get quite emotional if their religion is denigrated in any way. I have been forgiving of other religions, figuring one was as good as another. However, I have lately been noticing the damage that religions do, not only to the adherents, but also to the planet. Of course, there are also many positive effects of the religions, but I am focusing on the negative effects.

A couple examples: making rules about sex creates a bit of stress in peoples' lives; and the sacredness of a human life is causing an overpopulated planet. How about the power of positive thinking which causes missed opportunities and creates a lot of unnecessary guilt. Even the Eastern religions which suppress desire to alleviate pain cause people to curtail an important part of life, ecstasy.

A person who is limited in their creativity by laws or cultural rules or religious guilts will feel frustration, which can then bubble out into other areas of expression, negatively.

Meta-Religion

I started wondering what would life be like if we could do a complete reset, forget all the religions of the past, start over. I realize this isn't possible at this time, too many beliefs embedded deeply into the cultures and laws, but what if?

The basic premise here is that other religions rely on unprovable ideas, which means that they are belief-systems, not facts. So why can't I make my own belief-system and include unprovable ideas? One belief-system is as true as any other if unprovable. The big differences will be from the implications of the beliefs.

There is a method utilized in creating this belief-system. The only facts used are scientific and provable. Of course, if the science changes, there will have to be modifications. After that I do a great deal of speculation, but I try not to present ideas from books as fact, but as my logical extensions of the scientific facts. The ideas need to flow one from the other in a way that makes sense, and even though not provable, they feel right and fit with experience.

You will find many other writings in MetaShifting based on books and teachings, but they are not included in Wilderism as fact.

Implications

The main thrust of Wilderism is to change the focus of humans from themselves to their environment, to put the planet as the most important concept, to live in harmony with nature, not necessarily in harmony with each other, although that would be nice.

One of my great fears is that Wilderism will be modified to allow some people to feel superior to others. My design is that this belief-system will provide guidelines for making decisions, not absolute rules. There must be the compassion to understand that everyone is coming from a different place and that their decision will be based on their current situation. We need to "walk a mile in their moccasins" before judging them.

This will be almost impossible since some people's self-worth comes from comparing themselves to others, and if they feel like they fall short, then the easiest solution is to blame someone else. A feeling of self-worth must come from within, comparing ourselves today against yesterday, not comparing to others.

There are many ideas included which are controversial today and will stir up a lot of scorn, ridicule, and enmity. There is almost no hope of changes to the laws of countries to accommodate Wilderism. Therefore, this belief-system is not for today, but for a distant future.

Adherents

These ideas are meant to be followed by responsible adults who can make good decisions. It would not be healthy to ignore existing laws.

Preview

This document is pretty long-winded and is obvious in many places, so boring to many readers. But don't miss the "No Magic" section where I develop Spirit Guides, and the "Expand Consciousness" section includes my experiences with psychedelics.

REALITY IS

Objective Reality

In this day of computer-generated games and virtual reality, it is encouraging to think that your mind can invent and control reality. This gets to the heart of the human problem, that we think that we are superior to nature. We can manipulate reality to conform to our wishes. And to some extent, this is true. But then we lose sight of the reality, and that causes problems.

There are scientists who say that reality is constructed in the brain. While that may be true about the perception of reality, it still doesn't change the physics of events, objective-reality. Just try to move something with your mind. Then try to make someone else do something just by willing it. Ok, now really focus. Use your internal emotions, guts. No luck? That's REALITY you are trying to change. And by the way, anyone who tells you that you just didn't believe hard enough, well, that is the oldest blame game in the world---but it works because some people can be convinced of their own guilt and because it's not provable. "Gaslighted!"

Good vs Evil

I was raised in Christian Science, and that is all about "Know the Truth, and the Truth shall set you Free". It's on the front wall of the church. Evil only exists because you allow evil into your mind. I was excused from taking biology in high school because it included the study of diseases.

This gets to the heart of western religions, and that is that there is a good and evil, absolutely. Of course, metaphysics explains that good and evil are not absolute, but relative, depending on the point of view---not only who is looking at it, but from what standpoint.

For instance, a hurricane can destroy houses and cause power outages, a bad thing for the owners. However, the electrical workers in the next state have now got good paying overtime jobs fixing the wires, a good thing.

And then there is the time range viewpoint, a lucky win at the poker table may be followed by the loss of a wife for too much time at the casino. Good and evil are relative.

Metaphysics says that good and evil are the opposite sides of a single coin. When you create one, you automatically create the other. There is no such thing as good without evil. Defining one, creates the other, by definition. It is not necessary for us as humans to go through this process. It is possible to take things as they come, not bothering to classify them in terms of good and evil.

But the downside of this practice is that one can become accepting of anything, and we will go into that later.

Positive Thinking

To change the subject slightly, I have spent many an hour stoned on marijuana. I have checked, but not everyone has the same experiences I do, which is that I see meaning in nature. This is called "claircognizance". Things take on an importance not seen while straight. I really enjoy that state, but I have learned that when I come down, nothing around me has changed despite my mental gyrations.

In other words, REALITY IS.

It can't be changed with the mind. There is no point in "positive thinking" for changing things for the better.

However, "positive thinking" is valuable for staying happy, which is important for health. And don't forget the "placebo effect". Thinking we are healthy can help to actually making our bodies healthy. But that is not changing reality, just an effect of the mind/body interface.

Prayer

Science is the exploration and discovery of reality. We think we understand how something works and have to test it. If the result is as expected every time, then the theory is proven. But if it works sometimes, but not others, well then there must be a hidden variable not taken into account. So, we scratch our heads and say "how about this?". A scientist will then modify the experiment controlling for the new variable. This process continues until we truly understand.

So where does prayer come in? From what I have experienced and seen, prayer sometimes works and sometimes doesn't. There must be a hidden variable. What? We'll get to that with the No Magic tenet.

Gaia

The larger picture that this first tenet draws attention to is nature itself. If this planet has a consciousness, we call it Gaia. We as humans are created by nature, surrounded by nature, the forests and land and the sea, and filled with nature internally in the forms of microbes, bacteria, and viruses. The joke is: who is really in charge, the myriad bacteria that live in our guts, or us as a human? Are we just a support system for the bacteria? Which is more important? Naturally we think we are. Major egos.

But when we forget that we are part of Gaia, that's when we cause problems, not only for ourselves, but for the planet.

The name "Wilder" comes from the English, meaning someone who lives in the woods, a wilder. To me that indicates a person who is close to nature, a desirable trait. In the city, it is easy to forget that we are part of nature. After all, if we run out of money and food, someone is sure to take care of us. But out in the woods, you had better learn how to get food or you will starve, and learn how to make shelter also, not to mention protecting yourself from the pests and parasites.

The Native-Americans and indigenous peoples everywhere seem to have figured it out pretty well, living with nature and respecting it. Then the Europeans came along with the view of conquering nature. Not sustainable it turns out, what with global warming and the resultant droughts and food shortages. It appears humans are a self-correcting species, as are all species. When it gets to be too many for nature, there will be reductions.

This tenet is about recognizing the truth in which we live.

If we were going to define "good" and "bad", let's make it about what is good for the planet versus what is bad, as opposed to only thinking about that concept for ourselves. I am not saying to ignore our own desires, but to be aware of the cost. "Carbon Footprint" has become a concept which is useful for the planet. I would say let's go farther, let's say "Planetary Footprint".

Planetary Footprint

It would be beneficial to have a new profession of Planetary-Monitors, people who are trained to look at a situation or practice and who could give it a number. Then at least we could know what our footprint is, and make intelligent choices about what we have to have and what we can let go. The beauty of this is that it will be based on science, not on politics or outdated religions. I can see a new major in college where "Planetaries" become educated.

There should be a tax based on the size of a person's planetary footprint. If you need a big house with lots of extra rooms, fine, but it should cost more. Heating and cooling a large house should not only cost more in the heating and cooling expenses, but in the tax. This would encourage smaller living quarters. Perhaps the homeless who live in tents are a positive wave for the future and should be applauded, small planetary-footprint.

Everything purchased should have an indication of its planetary-cost, and not just the cost of manufacturing and distributing, but also the cost to the planet, and could be taxed accordingly. The tax would go to restoring the damage to the planet caused by that product.

Building a shopping mall would have a large footprint and should be taxed so that when the mall dies, it can be put back to nature, the parking lot and buildings razed and trees and grass replanted.

Even if there are no planetary taxes, there should at least be greater awareness. The idea is to start considering the planet when deciding what to do. We need to get closer to nature, if not in living, at least in our thinking.

Do you remember when the Pandemic started in 2020? What was the item which caused panic-buying? Do you remember that the stores finally said that a person could only buy one pack of toilet paper? Toilet paper! Now what does this indicate? To me it shows just how far removed we have become from nature. I certainly agree that cleanliness is desirable, but by what techniques? Toilet paper is made from felled trees, trees which create the oxygen which we need to breathe. And for what? To keep our hands clean? Can't get our hands dirty anymore? That's how far we have become estranged from nature. It has gotten to the point where public toilets must be self-flushing because people are afraid to touch a handle for a second---don't want to catch germs. Too far removed from nature in my opinion. A little soap and water handle these situations quite well. Not to mention that infants need to be exposed to dirt to develop a healthy immune system.

Overpopulation

Obviously, the old Biblical phrase "Be fruitful and multiply" is no longer a good idea. Even if we reduce our footprints, there are just too many people on the planet.

A lot of what is causing that is the third-world country concept of old-age insurance, lots of kids. Social security is a good idea for those countries.

Then there is the Catholic Church, which says that sex without trying to make a baby is wrong, and that birth-control and abortions are bad. Not helpful.

Even the medical profession is not helping by trying to save everybody. "Human life is sacred". I disagree. The planet is "sacred" and we are part of the planet, but not more important.

It used to be that Africans had natural birth control, a proportion of the babies would not survive. It is much easier on everybody when babies die than when they are older. A lot of philanthropic money has been spent reducing baby deaths in Africa, just to cause worse problems later housing and feeding everyone.

Birth-control and abortions should be free and easy to get. To avoid abortions, morning-after pills should be in every woman's purse. Sex is a natural act and cannot be stopped, shouldn't be, it is not only fun, but also a powerful urge. The thing is, a child shouldn't be the result. Of course, if someone or a couple wants a baby, fine, but no more accidental children.

Ending Life

Then there is the other end of birth, dying. It should be made painless and easy. Keeping someone alive beyond the point where life has meaning is not healthy for the planet. I recognize how the Hippocratic-Oath, to do no harm, is useful for the health-profession, but it is too absolute. There needs to be some balancing morality, or at least some other profession that helps in the dying process. A hospice helps with the discomfort of dying, but would be better if it could speed death up.

Kurt Vonnegut in his novels, advocated for suicide-parlors with purple roofs, right across the street from the then ubiquitous, orange-roofed Howard Johnsons. You could walk in and not walk out. You got your tasty last meal, whatever drug you wanted to get high, favorite music and scenes, go to sleep pleasantly, and not wake up.

Let those who have fulfilled their purpose in life leave room for those who have more to do. I am sure there will have to be some restrictions on who can do this, but it is a concept which will help the planet.

Dan Brown wrote his novel "Inferno", after his "The Da Vinci Code" and "Angels and Demons". It was about an "evil" genius they were trying to stop from distributing his manufactured virus. It turns out that the virus went global before they could stop it, and what it did was permanently change everyone's DNA so that only one out of every three people could make a baby.

Of course, Ron Howard couldn't put population-control in his "Inferno" movie, so it was bastardized to be about terrorists. Interesting---population-control is a taboo subject. No wonder we are in trouble. All biological species go through a period of population reduction when overpopulated.

Burial

What to do with our bodies when no longer needed? Egyptians and Christians like to preserve the body even after death, so preservatives like formaldehyde are pumped in and caskets and cemetery space used. Next cremation seems advisable, but it uses between 20 and 30 gallons of gasoline to completely burn a human body, 60% water.

I like the natural-burial, just a shroud covering my unpreserved body laid under a middle-aged magnolia tree. A young tree might not live and an old one will die sooner, so let my body feed a grown magnolia tree so that I can smell good to passersby for 60 years. I wouldn't mind a brass plaque nailed to the tree, "Here returns Chris Wilder, 1946 – 20??, Wilderist".

Personal Honesty

What I have been discussing is the impact to the planet, how we should become honest about the costs. Now let's change focus to ourselves, a single individual. Let's get honest.

We as a species are the evolutionary end-result of a bunch of other species---we are a part of nature to start with. It is true that we have imaginations which seem to be missing in other species, but we still don't understand where that came from, the simple higher number of neurons in our brains or aliens modifying our DNA. You can choose if you want, but I think the jury is still out, and it really doesn't matter---we have to deal with who we are.

Honesty. We should start at the most basic level. To survive as a member of this species, we must figure out how to eat and not get killed. Second, we must have sex to continue the species. Sex is quite basic, but our imaginations allow us to put all kinds of rules on it which might or might not be useful---that's called culture.

Why would we ask a human to deny his needs, hungers, urges? Unless of course, the need impacts someone else's life directly in a negative way. But otherwise, why would we?

Sexual Honesty

The scientists have come up with 3 aspects of sex: 1) what sexual equipment you are born with, 2) how you feel inside (male or female), and 3) which sex you are attracted to. It's not so simple, but it is basic. Of course, there are all the variations and the only judging that we can do would be based on the percentages, which ones are more prevalent. Lucky you if you should be born with the 2 "normal" aspect combinations, one being a female body feeling female and desiring males.

But what of the others? Do we call them "bad", "abnormal"? No. Diversity is a desirable attribute in nature, healthier in the long run. The coming out of LGBT people is a major step forward in a culture. And everyone is different in some way. If we can overcome the shame involved in being different, then we can be honest to others about ourselves, and that reduces stress, which means we will live longer healthier lives.

The Tail

I understand where it comes from, but sexual taboos have caused enormous stresses on most of our cultures. I realize that it is a very personal and even secret thing between 2 adults, but what is the problem with prostitution? There are many men who need it and lots of women who are happy to do it. The reverse also.

Of course it shouldn't be coerced in any way, but that is a different story. Thinking about it in relation to Gaia, prostitution has a smaller planetary footprint than marriage. Wives require a lot more amenities (washers, driers, etc.) than most men. In any case, sex shouldn't be the driving force in marriage, love and companionship should be.

The problem that a sex-starved man has is that his imagination can run away with him allowing him to believe that the woman he is after, really wants it. This leads to stalking and rape. There are also women who can fantasy about a recalcitrant man, leading to trouble.

It used to be that only men were the crew on ships. Now women are crew also. The testosterone of the men near a female goes up, this is biology. Most men can control it, but some, not possible. That's why I think there should be prostitutes aboard every ship.

This is not my idea. It comes from a 6-book series written by Piers Anthony called "The Bio of a Space Tyrant". He had it so that a space-ship about to embark on a months-long or years-long voyage would advertise in the paper for prostitutes to come aboard. They were paid by the company and their job was to take care of the sexual needs of the crew in order to keep them stress-free. It was always a joke among the beginner crewmen that they were going to "wear out *the tail*". Of course, it couldn't be done.

Status

Another source of dishonesty are the clothes and jewelry we wear. People judge others by those things, but do they really indicate who we are, or just what we have? Wilderism supports the idea of nudist colonies because when you are not afraid to show your "imperfect" body to others, you are coming to grips with who you really are, imperfections and all. I'll show you my imperfections if you will show me yours. And by the way, if you have ever been to a nudist colony, you realize that the experience is not about sex, it is about the suspension of judgment of others. Can you be that honest?

Science Misunderstood

Science itself goes through times when it is misunderstood, and this is understandable. Science has different branches. We call physics and chemistry "hard" sciences meaning that the laws are well defined and work every time, while biology is more "soft" because there are so many variables due to evolution changing things all the time, psychology very "squishy" because of the highly variable nature of the brain and consciousness, and lastly we get to nutrition, which shouldn't be called a science at all.

Many people don't trust science because of the news reports, that this "new discovery turns physics on its head!". What they don't realize is that the physics that is being discovered is for the very small or the very large. At our level of space, speed, and time, physics laws were set down by Newton back in 1687 and still apply perfectly today. Yes, when it comes down to elementary particles or galaxies, there are changes in the theories going on, but at our level everything is understood and works, otherwise TVs, cellphones, and computers couldn't be trusted. So blame the misunderstanding on journalists who need to excite with a splashy headline about "new science".

And as far as nutrition is concerned, every couple years somebody comes up with a theory about how to eat more healthy. They publish books, do talks, TV shows, and DVDs. They make a bunch of money and most people follow along like a herd of sheep. Of course, this new diet or whatever, only works on some people, not even on most. And then a couple years later along comes another "genius". Nutrition has to do with how people absorb food, but there are so many different variations of human, that one-size never fits all. Nutrition is not a science, it's more like an endless series of fads.

SUSTAINABLE ECSTASY

Definition

"Ecstasy" is the state of consciousness involving happiness, a lot of happiness---the release of endorphins and other mood enhancers in the brain.

There are thousands of ways to get ecstatic and every individual has their own unique set of methods, kind of like a fingerprint. There's good food, good sex, drugs, love, and any kind of creativity which makes us happy. There are also meditation, gambling, sports, and music.

Nature naturally awards good behavior and punishes bad behavior. The reward is in the form of happiness, laughter. The punishment is pain. Therefore, to go with the flow of nature, one should look to what makes us happy. It is a process of discovery because nobody tells us as kids what those things are. Our parents can show us their own happiness, which is highly important, but should not be construed to be our own happiness. I have found that when I watch myself and find happiness, if I focus on it and submit to it, it has branches coming from it, other possibilities and variations, ad infinitum. Following ecstasy is like growing trees, each trunk leading to branches, some more powerful than others. Follow the best. Ecstasy is a process which continues an entire lifetime, getting more and more refined and tuned to only ourselves. Build your ecstasy trees.

Drugs are good, but they are enhancers of ecstasy which borrow from the future. Expect a payment, and that's ok as long as you can accept the cost.

Addiction

The big problem with any ecstasy is that it can become addictive.   This is especially a problem for those with addictive personalities. Most people can stop having fun when it is no longer appropriate, but there are others who can't quit. One of the problems with a culture is that it makes rules based on the bad experiences of the addictive, forcing the "normal" people to abandon some forms of ecstasy. This leaves people anxious and unsatisfied, which causes other problems in the culture.

That is where "sustainable" comes in. A person who is not addictive knows when to quit and take on the responsibilities of living. Can you get high today and do it again tomorrow? Sustainable.

For those who are addicted to some form of ecstasy, so far there isn't any solution except to stay away from it. The 12-step programs sometimes work, but again they are basically building up the will to say no to the drug. I wonder if there are better techniques than abstinence. Whatever, again it is a process of self-discovery---which ecstasies can I play with, and which ones are dangerous for me. That's what I call the real adventure of life, exploring my own set of ecstasies.

Needs

To get more detailed, let's examine Maslow's Hierarchy of Needs:

Physiological

Safety

Belonging and Love

Esteem

Cognitive

Aesthetic

Self-Actualization

Transcendence

The theory is that once a lower need is taken care of, then it is possible to move up to the next higher need. It is hard to work on Esteem if Safety is being threatened. Of course, some people may decide to skip levels and there is no reason that multiple levels can't be attempted at the same time.

Progress

Success at each level delivers endorphins, which is what keeps us trying to improve our lives. Taking basic biology, it is in the nature of cells that when the conditions are beneficial, it is time to split. In other words, when a level is complete, the endorphins are reduced and can be regained by going to the next level. So progress is built not only into biology, but also into consciousness in general.

It isn't only need-achievements which release endorphins, there are some things that are more direct. Eating is naturally high producing. Sex is great. Drugs go right to the source in the brain. Wilderism promotes all of these, the more the better. But in a balanced way. There are responsibilities involved in just living, and focusing on endorphin production only is not sustainable. Take care of business first, then there will be time for the higher pursuits.

This is very important. Metaphysics says that if you ignore what is being requested of you, it won't go away and will limit your time to get high. Pay attention to what or who requires your attention now, satisfy it as soon as possible, and then you will be free to work on your pleasures.

Pleasures

As mentioned before, a personal pleasure is like a branch on a tree with many smaller more detailed branches coming from it. Enlarge the branch you are on, look at the smaller branches for what excites you, and then spend time enhancing that branch, and on and on. It is a form of creativity, the creativity leading to becoming more and more who you are, more defined as you get older. It's kind of fun!

But don't forget sustainable.

Pain

Now let's look at pain. This is nature saying, "don't go this way." Note however that there are some pains that are translated into ecstasy, kinky things---that's different. For some people, the greatest ecstasies are the result of pain from the one you love.

First there is the pain from just having a body, especially as it slows down when you get older.

Second is the pain from making a bad decision.

And third is the pain from paying back karma.

For the first body pain, there may be exercises or procedures that can be done to reduce the pain, possibly medical things. All of these are worth trying, some with limited success. I have found that as I get older, there are parts of my body that require attention that weren't needed before. These things take time and money, and at some point, they will overwhelm the pleasures. For me, when that happens it will be time to exit this body. No longer worth it. According to metaphysics, I'll get a new one. Wilderism is in favor of suicide, hopefully pleasant and not messy.

The karmic pain is easier to deal with if you realize that that is what it is. Then you may be able to aid the process and speed it up. Just work through it as quickly as possible. How can you tell if the pain is from karma? Not too hard. Just think of the other 2 reasons for pain and if it is neither of those, it is probably karmic.

The second pain is the easiest to deal with. Just change whatever decision led to it---if you can. I have had many decisions which I wasn't sure which way to go, so I just chose one and watched the results, pleasure or pain. Then I knew. Many times, it isn't too late to reverse course, and even if it is too late, there is the learning which comes from it. Don't do it again.

I have been reminded that there is another kind of pain, the pain of compassion. This is when empathy kicks in and you feel the pain another person is going through. This pain is selective, in other words you can choose to feel it or not and can choose who to feel it for. We couldn't survive if we felt it for everyone.

Meditation

Meditation is another good method of achieving ecstasy. I try to have a yoga/meditation session several times a week. I do my own modified Kripalu Yoga flow for 15 minutes followed by transcendental meditation for 15 minutes.

The yoga gets my body into a calm state through stretching muscles and relaxing them---a lot of deep controlled breathing. It isn't the primary purpose, but the yoga also helps my physical body, especially in old age. I have incorporated some physical therapy positions in my yoga flow.

Then the meditation. I let my breath dwindle down to almost nothing and focus on my mantra. There are 4 stages in transcendental meditation: 1) meditating, 2) monkey chatter, 3) realization of monkey chatter, and 4) getting back to meditation, in a continuous cycle. I have found that I can enhance the ecstasy by visualizing waves of pleasure sweeping slowly across my brain.

I believe that one of the major results of practicing meditation is the ability to control the brain. The quote I like is, "The brain is an excellent tool, a horrible master." Having the ability to stop the brain when it is headed in a paranoid direction is very useful, and leads to a life of peace.

Love

Love is a great ecstasy, basically the desire to be with someone or something. It not only releases endorphins in the brain, but also oxytocin, the love hormone. If it is shared between two people, it creates feelings that are like no other. In the beginning of a love relationship, it is capable of extending consciousness beyond the body and mind into super ecstasy. There are many internal and external benefits in loving.

Naturally, like anything else, love has a negative side because it can turn to pain and hatred, either through exploitation or rejection. As an image, I like to think of standing balanced on my own 2 feet, then leaning over to the loved one, so that if they move away, I won't fall over. On the other hand, I believe in combining our talents letting one partner take over where they are stronger. Doing everything as equals seems a waste of talents.

Sex

Now let's talk about sex. People accuse me of "having sex on the brain". And it's true. I do. Why? Because it is so easy to shock people when talking about it. Plus, I think having sex is even better than good food at releasing endorphins. Just my experience. Another thing, it is a great way to share with someone, not that that is necessary.

There are many variations of discussions about sex, all the way from those who don't want to talk about it at all to those who can't help sharing everything. There are some sex subjects that are taboo, and some allowed. How did this happen? How did sex become a dirty word? The prohibition about sex seems to have arisen with the 2 main Western religions, Christianity and Islam. Before them the Romans had lots of fun. In the East, there is Tantric Yoga, where their bible enumerates the various positions.

Maybe the unease is about how animalistic it becomes if done right. For those who need to believe that humans are "better" than animals, sex is a throwback. To let go of your sophistication and get loud and messy, can't be handled by those who need to think of themselves as "better". Why do they need that? Because they are afraid it is not true in their case. I like the story of the hippie couple living in an old church building up in New England; after sex, he would ring the church bell---let the whole town know. I suppose it would get kind of noisy if everyone did that. On the other hand, there are those who don't get any thrill from sex at all, and that is ok too. The point is to figure out who you are with it.

Fantasies

There are those who have no imagination when it comes to sex, no creativity. They still like it, but "vanilla" sex is fine for them. The creative kinky ones generally fall into two categories: dominant and submissive, some people switching between them. From my experience we are born with that. It arises in the form of fantasies, which by the way, is another excellent way to release endorphins. Like the tree analogy, fantasies can be explored, also getting more and more detailed with time.

Real nirvana occurs when you can find someone else to share your fantasies. And if love is involved, it gets much more ecstatic because each partner is trying to enhance the experience for the other. I don't know how sex can be good the first time, because usually it takes learning about each other's fantasies to get it right. Then when that happens, it is possible to merge fantasies and let them grow.

Variations. That's what it is all about. Some things get us excited, and some don't. But whatever it is, allow yourselves to explore fantasies and then act on them, sustainably of course. There is no wrong sex act as long as it isn't done in a hurtful way, unless the agreed on kinky hurt induces ecstasy also.

Drugs

All drugs should be legal and easy to get. Making laws against drugs just creates a whole criminal class and demeans laws in general. Rock-climbing can be dangerous but should not be illegal. Taking drugs to get high can be dangerous too. It depends on which drugs and how much taken. We can't put a fence around every cliff, and we can't protect everyone from every drug. So just make sure that the education is out there to describe the dangers of every drug and put into place good treatment clinics which can deal with those who go beyond their own limits.

Some drugs are physically addictive, hard to quit. Those drugs release dopamine as well as endorphins. Dopamine production in the brain requires more and more to get high. It becomes a downward spiral. Some people can break free of this, and some can't. But just because some things are addictive doesn't mean that they should be banned. One part of human nature is the desire to get high and just because a particular drug is injurious to some doesn't mean it will be bad for all.

Humiliation

If a person has permanent damage from a drug, that is just the price for the ecstasy. What about death? Question: which comes first, the downward-spiral drug or the lack of self-respect which accepts the danger from the drug? There are some people who don't care if they go down into humiliation, so let them go. It is ok. There is no need to save everyone. There are too many people on the planet anyway.

This is the way of nature. When there are too many of any species, there is a culling. Just because we are humans doesn't mean that we can escape the laws of nature, the laws of biology.

MINIMIZE KARMA

Definition

I want to first give you my definition of "karma". It is whatever violates the natural flow of events.

If someone is walking toward me on the sidewalk and about to pass, but I step in front of them for no reason, that creates karma. If on the other hand, I suddenly see that I am about to step into a hole and step in front of them, no karma.

Suppose I am motoring my dinghy in the harbor and about to pass a rowboat with a fisherman. I would slow down if I was going to upset them. But first I would look behind me to see what kind of wake I was developing, and if small, I wouldn't slow down. Sometimes slowing down produces a bigger wake. In either case, I am going to rock them a bit, so some karma is created, but not much. I would do whatever would minimize the karma created.

The other factor is the cost to pay back the karma. Sometimes I don't want to follow the flow because I don't like where I see it going. In that case I can use "free won't" and go against the flow, but I would have to be aware of the cost, be willing to pay it back later. That's the other part of karma, it needs to be paid back.

Physics

Remember that the definition of "metaphysics" is "the unifying principles of science, religion, and philosophy". So of course the "religious" concept of karma must have a counterpart in physics. It is called Hamilton's Principle.

This major principle in physics states that in any closed system (non-outside interference), the potential and kinetic energies of the system will tend to be equal.

The easiest graphic example is the pendulum. At rest the pendulum is at the bottom, so no potential energy, and it is also not moving so no kinetic energy. They are equal.

Now pull the pendulum to the side and up and hold it. The potential energy is now the distance to the bottom, but the kinetic energy is still zero. This is an unnatural state due to an outside influence, the hand holding the pendulum.

Let it go. According to the laws of physics, the kinetic energy will build up and potential energy will reduce until they are equal. This does indeed occur, about half way down. But after that, the kinetic energy continues to grow while the potential reduces down to zero, at the bottom. This is due to momentum, the moving pendulum just can't stop on a dime.

Now at the bottom the potential energy is zero, but the kinetic energy is at the maximum. Again Hamilton's Principle comes in. The kinetic needs to be reduced to equal the potential, which again occurs halfway up. But momentum continues to influence the pendulum until kinetic goes to zero while the potential is maximized. This "tendency" to equals will continue forever except for outside forces like air-resistance.

Generalize this to a planet's orbit around its star. The potential is the gravitational attraction between the 2 bodies, and the kinetic is the speed the planet has around the star. It turns out that when measured, the kinetic and potential energies are equal.

Now to return to metaphysics, let's make an analogy to a living being. if in our life we are more active (kinetic) than our potential, this is creating karma and the system we are in will "tend" to reduce the active down to the potential, but due to momentum we may overshoot that point and our activities may reduce too far. Depending on the situation, that could be considered a "nervous breakdown".

Ideally then, what we want is to have our activity level match our potential at every moment, then no karma is created.

Types of Karma

Did you notice that there was no mention of "bad" karma? That is because advanced-metaphysics postulates that both "good" and "bad" karma exist.

"Good" karma is when you help someone who shouldn't be helped, thus slowing their process of growth. What it means is that sometime in the future (next lifetime?) you will have to be the recipient of an equal amount of "good" karma, someone helping you in a situation where you don't need it. This can take you out of your natural flow.

Obviously "bad" karma should be avoided---taking someone else out of their natural flow for your own gain.

But it is hard to categorize any particular act with karma, because if the act is within the natural flow at the time, then no karma is produced. If you hurt someone who is about to hurt you, no karma, also depending on the level of hurt.

Decisions

It's all about decisions. Given an event which will require a decision, karma should be a part of what is decided.

Most of the time, the next step to be taken is obvious and there is no reason to not go along with it.

What does the situation require?

It is said that the cost is equal to the disturbance, but that it doesn't need to be paid back to the same person. The desirable option would be to incur the cost sooner than later, so 1) it isn't left hanging, and 2) it might be possible to learn something from the experience. It seems that "the good die young". Maybe because they don't have any karma. Maybe those with evil intentions can put off paying the karma until next lifetime. That would explain babies born into unfortunate circumstances---left with no choice about whether to pay the karma now or not.

Back to "good karma", before you help someone, examine your own motives. If you feel genuine compassion and you have the means to help, then no karma is produced. However if there is a feeling of superiority or a need to appease self-guilt, then watch out.

Working Off Karma

What is the mechanism enforcing the payment of karma? I'll leave that for the next tenet.

But I will say now that the indication that we are working off karma is this: is there some kind of physical, emotional, or mental pain that we are going through that is not because of a bad decision or old age? An out of the blue type of thing. And not imaginary either. Could be short or long lasting.

A Wilderist looks at someone who is having a hard time and wonders what caused that karma, and appreciates the suffering the other is going through even while knowing that it is beneficial for the soul. And of course, if possible and in the flow, a Wilderist could try to reduce the other's suffering. However, sometimes the suffering is important, so it would be a mistake to fix it. I usually go by how I feel at the moment of my decision, no hard and fast rule.

Class

It has been shown that as far as intelligence and skills and drive, there is no difference between people based on skin color, religion, gender, or anything else. Every individual should be given the same opportunities as any other. What is done with the opportunities will of course be varied. A class system has no place in Wilderism.

NO MAGIC

Diseases

I keep thinking about the Middle Ages and the diseases they encountered. They had no idea what caused them, so speculated that it was evil thoughts, which resulted in a lot of innocent people being tortured and killed.

The microscope was invented around 1600 by Zacharias Janssen, a Dutch eyeglass maker. That revealed a world of living creatures unknown until then. In 1861 Louis Pasteur developed modern germ theory, proving that tiny bacteria were causing disease. In 1928 penicillin, the first antibiotic, was discovered by Alexander Fleming allowing humans to get control over bacteria. In the 1960s the first antiviral drugs were invented, getting control of specific viruses, which are much smaller than bacteria. In 2020, MRNA technology was used to allow for a safer vaccine, using cells to manufacture the spikes of Covid so that our bodies would develop a resistance to the real virus.

Today most religions promote a belief that incorrect thought is creating our misfortunes. Basically, the Power of Positive Thinking.

Psychic World

But what if there is another unknown world out there? One we haven't discovered yet. Some label this world the "psychic", magical thoughts, knowledge. The world of physics is ruled by elementary particles flying around. The psychic world is ruled by what? Thoughts? Prayers? Ghosts? Sounds like the Middle Ages to me. At least we aren't torturing and killing people now. Or are we?

When I was in college I got a Bachelor of Science in physics, in which I totally believe---there is a lot of proof for science. This computer is a result of applied physics. "Proof" means that it works every time and if it doesn't, there is some other variable we are missing. Science is based on provable facts.

I also believed in ghosts and psychic things, but no proof. My final physics paper was "The Relationship Between Elementary Particles and Ghosts". My physics advisor said I needed to get it out of my system and the other physics professor just laughed through my presentation. I think I got an "A" on the paper, but what I demonstrated was that there was no relationship, that physics works in space and time and that the psychic seems to ignore distances and time. There was evidence of thoughts being transmitted around the world ignoring the impossibility of science to explain it. But of course, no proof. There are those who seem to have more psychic ability than others, but when brought into the laboratory for proof, usually their gift works once and after that it is random. No proof.

Coincidences

Now let's switch to my own experiences. When I examine my life, there are obvious "miracles". In the last few decades, there was the coincidence of meeting my wife, Yani, in Indonesia in 1991, a woman obviously my next wife and we are still married today. There was also the coincidence of finding Magus in 2002, our ready to go sailboat, in Florida in one week---a lot of boat owners search for years.

My life is full of these coincidences, so many in fact that I have coined a phrase, "THERE ARE TOO MANY COINCIDENCES TO BE A COINCIDENCE".

This is my "jumping off point" for the existence of Spirit Guides.

Something is going on, and it isn't physics. We are more than billiard balls bouncing around randomly. And I am not talking about our control over our actions, I am talking about the stuff that happens to us not through any mechanisms we caused, the "accidents", the "lucky or unlucky streaks", "miracles"--- the "I didn't see it coming" types of events. Not to mention the protections.

Causes

There are those who refuse to acknowledge any type of external intelligent influence and just take life as it comes, not thinking about the why's. And that is ok. The "unexamined life" it is called. There is nothing wrong with that, keeps things simple and real, no illusions.

And then there are those who ascribe any unexpected events to God or Jesus or whatever god or goddess or spirit is believed in. And that is fine too. What's in a name? It is the looking outside of oneself that is important. The problem comes in when the belief system becomes relied upon instead of taking actions on one's own. Then it becomes a crutch and demeans being alive.

For me, I am always looking for the "behind the scenes" machinations. "What is going on?" I have examined lots of belief systems, and other than science, there doesn't seem to be any proof. If you have actually seen Jesus, can you help me to see him too? Not without faith. And faith is, by definition, the absence of proof.

Belief Systems

What can I believe in without proof? That is the question I have been asking. Everyone wants to be "in the know" and to have a safety factor others don't have, an advantage. That is what religions are generally about. "I believe in my religion and sorry about that, but yours is false and won't save you." That conclusion has led to a lot of persecution and wars.

What do I do? Too many coincidences and no proofs. Obviously, I have to accept an existing belief system or, in my case, invent a new one. I have always believed in "reinventing the wheel", so a new one it is.

Physics

And this is where Wilderism will leave a lot of people behind, where it gets too fantastic to believe. But the following is necessary to get rid of the "magic". This belief system was developed not through divine inspiration, but through logic.

Physics shows that there are millions of neutrinos passing through our bodies every second, all without an interaction. Most of them pass straight through the Earth also. Their vibration levels are so high that they don't interact with the elementary particles which make up normal matter, much slower vibrations. Also, they don't have an electric charge, so aren't detectable directly. A metaphysical principle for vibration levels: LIKES ATTRACT LIKES. The point is that there is a lot of room within physics for entities to exist at a lot faster vibration than ours, not only faster frequencies, but also faster times, meaning they wouldn't be detectable using scientific instruments or our 5 physical senses.

Consciousness

What about consciousness? Since we don't know what consciousness actually is, it is possible that there can be those kinds of interactions between these faster beings and us---and that is what I think is happening. We can contact each other through thought. Seems like magic, but it isn't.

Obviously if these beings can set up coincidences, they must be intelligent---external forces seemingly intelligent. God would be good to explain it all, but to me in any decent organization, the big guy doesn't worry about the little details, he or she sets the tone and the direction. What about Jesus? Again, too many people are asking Jesus for help. I want someone more tuned to me only. Big ego again. Then there is the soul, the level of consciousness which accumulates our experiences from lifetime to lifetime. According to metaphysics, the soul decides to incarnate a human into time and space in order to experience certain things, maybe to learn, or maybe just to do something in a new way.   No proof, but yes, I can go with that.

Some scientists claim that consciousness is an emergent property, in other words, if you get enough neurons working together, consciousness springs up. I believe in the opposite, that the brain and body are manifestations of a consciousness. The human soul consciousness needs to experience everything, and incarnates bodies into space and time over and over again, accumulating the experiences.

Soul

Where did the belief in a soul come from? Maybe it is a "neatness" I need to have. There doesn't seem to be much point without the accumulation of experience and wisdom. Obviously one lifetime isn't enough. I have to believe in reincarnation and there must be an "accumulator" of experience and that is the soul.

I can't see it, can't prove it, but it makes sense that some (maybe all?) of whatever wisdom I have comes from other lifetimes.

Causes

The soul is setting a goal, a direction. What I need is a more immediate entity, someone who handles the nuts and bolts, creates the actual "coincidences". Think of the soul as the writer, us humans as the actors, and then the in-between guy, the director. That makes sense to me.

What to call this director? This goes back to the beginning of humans, as far as we know, the beliefs in spirits. Most ancient and some religions have spirit guides. I like that. The in-between intelligence that helps to implement the goals set by the soul and to guide a human. To abbreviate, "spirit guide" will be called "SG" from now on.

Spirit Guides

Any proof of SGs? No, but there is as much proof as any other religion. It's a belief-system, but for me it must have some ideals and a lot of pragmatism. It has to explain as much as possible without magic, the "deus ex machina" (act of god) that is so maligned in literature. Too easy. It needs to be useful in some way.

A human is necessary to interact with the physical. It is too difficult for a SG to do it all the time, too expensive in concentration and energy. The problem with the human is its body, which has the misfortune to be subject to pests and other physical ailments. Most religious belief systems give comfort to the sick in some way, if not actual help, then at least hope for a better future.

Wilderism doesn't do that. It can explain what is going on, which gives understanding, but no hope. That is why I think Wilderism is a failed belief-system, right off the bat. I'm fine with that.

What about the love that people have for God or Jesus? Can I love my SG? Maybe if she is beautiful and intelligent. Somehow that love falls by the wayside with Wilderism.

Prime Directive

Let's discuss what a SG looks like, and this is derived from a logical point of view, not actual experience from contact.

First, a SG has a prime directive which is very similar to the most important thing about being a voyeur. Don't get caught. Why? Two reasons. Obviously, there is the social tigma for being discovered of being a voyeur, but more importantly, it is true that when someone thinks they are being watched, they will cease to act naturally.

There are a range of responses when it is discovered that you are being watched: 1) continue to act as you would have, 2) act like you think you should, 3) show off, 4) stop doing anything at all, and 5) decide to rebel against the expected direction of action.

The point for the SG is that it is hard to know which of these choices will be taken---much simpler to just not get caught. And that means that it is important for the SG to not do anything which is provable with science. Leave them guessing. Or at least, even if experienced by the human directly, the vision can't be proven to be true by anyone else.

Manipulations

What can a SG do? The "urge" is the most cost-effective action. Put an urge into the human to do something. The human usually doesn't know where it comes from, and it can get the desired result. It is kind of a game for the SG. Figure out what will propel the human in the right direction. A planted thought? A noticed billboard? A dream?

And then there is the big one of getting two people together that have something to work out with each other, like marriage. That may require several urges over a long period of time, and for additional complication, coordinated with another SG on the other human.

The big advantage a SG has is that it can see the whole lifetime of the human, and pop in here and there in time to get the job done---the job the soul and human have agreed upon before birth.

Think of the movie "Groundhog Day". Bill Murray relived the same day over and over and knew what was going to happen. When asked if he was God, he said "No, I'm not that smart." He just knew the future---made him look like God. It looks like the SG is God, but he isn't that smart either.

There is a need to believe that SGs are pure, loving, and wise. Maybe some of them are. But all of them? What are they, clones? Intelligence doesn't work that way. Geniuses tend not to work together for very long, heading off in their own directions.

Divinely guided? Sounds pretty restrictive. Even more restrictive than us. Either higher entities are intelligent or they are automatons, or could be somewhere in between. Wisdom can't be anything but intelligent.

Functions

What can a SG do? Travel in the human's lifetime, plant urges, and if necessary, perform some actual physical manipulations. He definitely doesn't want to get caught doing that, so one-offs. Plus, the cost for changing the physical is way above just planting an urge or knowledge.

Think of the lucky streak a gambler has throwing dice or playing poker. If it is important for the human to win, that will require a bunch of changes in human real time. That implies that the SG can get in, make a change, and get out without being seen. That would only be possible if he could move so fast that not even scientific instruments can catch him. Pretty good, but it has got to be expensive energy wise, not done all the time. This also implies that the SG isn't going to be full time with the human because most of the time the human can operate well on its own.

Creativity

Most humans have a special area of creativity, maybe more than one. Music, art, inventions, healing. Whatever it is, you can ask a person where their creativity comes from and they will probably say "it is just there", they don't know. Sounds like a SG function.

Is there any reason why a human can't have several SGs working with them? Not that I can see. Maybe each SG has a special area of creativity.

God

Let's talk about God for a minute. What is it? What are the requirements? Obviously not male or female. How about good or evil? No, we already have shown that good and evil are not absolute concepts, but relative. How about a loving God? But we know that hate flourishes in humans, so God isn't too good with that one. And Vishnu, the god of the Hindus has two sides, one love and the other hate.

So what are the requirements for being God, or a god? Seems to me there are only a couple, one being that it is eternal, lives a long time, and the second, able to travel in our time, therefore capable of knowing things, not everything, just those things needed. This god doesn't have to be particularly smart, not moral in our sense of the word, not even have a good memory. Just able to travel in time! That is a simple definition of god. Anybody can be a god if they can jump around in time. Maybe the eternal is a little too much also. What if God gets changed every once in a while? It does seem that humans go through peaceful times punctuated by times of wars. Could it be a regime change?

What do you actually know about God? Nothing which someone hasn't told to us or something we read. On the other hand, what do you know of your SGs? You will probably say nothing. But I would say that we know a lot more than we realize. Think of all the times when something miraculous has happened to you, things not explainable otherwise. These could be negative things too. Those events actually show you who your SGs are, what they respond to and what they don't, which directions are important to them.   There's a personality involved.

Our Spirit Guides

What can we do as humans? I would say that we have creativity embodied in our own brains, but that sometimes it takes a "divine spark" to get it going in a particular direction. As an exercise, list all your special talents. Then assume that there is a different SG to guide us in each area, and give he, she, or it a name---any name is fine, male or female. Maybe even assign an imaginary face and a body to it. Then watch for the little urges and inspirations done by that SG so that you will come to know him/her/it.

The English language is so bad with pronouns. If I say "he", I am denying "she", so then I say "it", but that is so impersonal. I'll just use "he" or "she" depending on what that SG is capable of. Then I'll assign an appropriate name, knowing that it might not be accurate, but the SG doesn't care. Name and gender are fluid concepts for a SG.

Our Place

I prefer to think of the human/SG relationship as a "cooperation". I've got my own daily life to lead and there is no need for SG intervention. But sometimes events occur to me that are so subtle that I don't recognize them as SG manipulations. And then there are those events that are obviously a little extra, not totally from me.

Can a SG make a mistake? Sure, but being able to travel in our time, means that mistakes can be fixed. Do SG always have our best interests in mind? Yes, but what we think of as "best" may not be in the path needed to satisfy our life's mission. What is our life's mission? Hard to say, the SG doesn't usually reveal that to us. With our strong imaginations, it is not useful to know the future, can change it, make it harder to achieve the mission. Better not to know.

SG Doings

You could say that all of this is a lot fanciful, full of unneeded complications. True. And you could say that Occam's Razor applies here, that the simplest solution is the right one. However, Occam's Razor is not always correct. Look at

Quantum Mechanics, not simple at all, and certainly not intuitive, but definitely provable.

Another possibility: multiple personalities. Could be. But that doesn't explain the coincidence of two people finding each other.

If I were an intelligent creative SG, I'd want to talk to other SGs, compare notes like doctors do with each other. No names of course. "You won't believe what my human did today!" There must be places to get together, kind of like bars on Earth. Can't be working all the time, isn't needed. But a bar would require a bar tender. So not all spirits are guides.

I wonder if there is special training before a spirit can be become a SG. Probably. If nothing else, drumming-in the prime directive in would require a lot of teaching. A degree in SG'ing---lots of degrees, implying promotions and demotions. An entire civilization and culture of spirits. Not so simple, but natural for intelligent beings.

Another implication, not all spirits are helpful, some are malevolent. Metaphysics says to be careful about contacting spirits, be sure you have a "good" one, a real SG. Need to see a diploma or something. How to know? That is relatively simple, a higher spirit urging love, compassion, understanding or a lower entity encouraging hate, divisiveness, separation. Maybe these "negative" spirits are guides also, getting us into situations which we have determined to be useful before being born.

Actions

I believe that we as humans are being influenced by our SGs a lot. How many times have you read about someone being led to create something, inspired? And how many times have you heard of a killer saying, "I don't know what happened. I just wanted to talk to him." Are these events evidence of SGs taking over temporarily?

That leads to culpability. If my SG made me do it, is it really my fault? My answer to that is that we as humans must react to bad behavior as if SGs didn't exist. Otherwise, the civilization falls apart. And maybe going to prison is part of the plan my soul needed for me to experience this lifetime. It turns out that my cellmate is also my soul-brother.

Our Control

It would be interesting to see if we could figure out how to eliminate the negative SGs, or at least to intervene in those cases. But then we would be messing with the good/evil balance of life which is not only impractical but also not useful. It is the push and pull of life experiences which make it interesting and stimulates growth.

"KNOW THYSELF" is the quote from Socrates. But what about if I am a natural-born serial-killer with a psychopathic SG? Does just realizing that I am a serial-killer fix it? Or should I become the best serial-killer possible? That's where the third tenet comes in, minimize karma. Taking away someone else's ability to lead their own life creates karma, which is not good.

Nevertheless, I do believe we have some control. Obviously our SGs are going to try to get us to fulfill our life's mission. But what if we object, "No, no, not this lifetime". Possible? I think so. If SGs had total control, they would just say so and we would be relegated to puppet status. But no, they hide as much as possible from us in order that we make decisions on our own. It's a cooperation.

TAROT

One of the best ways to communicate with a SG is through a Tarot card reading.

For those of you who don't know, the Tarot cards have 21 major arcana and 4 suits of 14 cards each. Each card has a meaning with various interpretations. My favorite cards are the Waite deck loaded with picture symbolism, and my favorite book with accompanying meanings and interpretations is "Mastering the Tarot" by Eden Gray.

There are many methods, but I prefer the Celtic Cross layout with a Significator and 10 cards laid out, some of them upside down, or "reversed" which changes the meaning.

The way it works is for the seeker to shuffle their energy and question into the deck, then select out the cards turning them up one at a time until the 10 cards are in the cross. Then the reader interprets each card, using the book or not, and comes up with a story for the whole. There are many words said to the seeker, but only a few meanings will stick in the seeker's mind, and that is the message.

I have never found the cards to lie and usually they reveal things I don't know, maybe still don't know after the reading because unless told, I don't know which meanings hit home.

I have a SG I have named Kathy who is pretty amazing, and I am sure she works with the seeker's SG to provide the message most pertinent for the time.

From a SG's perspective, I bet they love a good Tarot reading because it can get across a complex and subtle message very quickly, easier than a series of planted urges and inspirations. And still no proof, so it's ok.

A warning needs to come at this point. Remember that "REALITY IS". Be careful of making radical changes to your life based on divination of whatever kind. Any change indicated by a reading should be viewed as possibly a wrong interpretation, and checked out for logical reasonableness, maybe a second opinion. You may want to ease into a change to see how it goes, and if it is incorrect and you experience pain---time to back off. On the other hand, if you experience pleasure after the decision, it could very well be a sign the decision was correct.

Note also that the Ouija Board is known as a means used by lower entities to get control for their own power trip. Be careful of a negative entity claiming to be an angel to trick you into a path of negativity. Don't give up your logic.

Psychopaths

What should a psychopath do when they realize they are a psychopath, and under the influence of a negative SG? Not sure. How to say "free-won't" when a SG can slip in and modify our actions without us realizing it? That's where I am now---don't know the answer. But I'll keep working on it.

A statistic I recently read is that every 1 out of a 1000 humans is genetically a psychopath. That means that the part of the brain involved in empathy is non-functional.

But why bring psychopaths up at all? Because they are at the top of many corporations and governments, and they don't always rule in a healthy way.

If you have no empathy, it also means that you are not afraid of what others worry about. No feelings, no fear. Whew! Like superman! Little-fear lends to big risk-taking, more than your average person, and this results in success for the psychopath when it comes to negotiating with a normal person. They naturally rise to the top. Rules for normal people don't apply to them. Thus they naturally run afoul of laws, which is why the prisons are loaded with psychopaths.

There are good psychopaths also---surgeons. We have a friend who became a surgeon like his father. After 3 years he changed professions. "Why?" we asked. "Because I got tired of seeing the good people die." This guy had feelings. It is a useful trait for a surgeon to be a psychopath.

We have another acquaintance who was hired by multiple companies to "clean house", in other words to fire a lot of people. Now he says he doesn't want any more of those jobs, even though they paid quite well. It finally caught up with him, having to let somebody go who had been with the company for 20 years and only had 2 more months until retirement. His compassion-pain finally rose to overflowing.

But not for a psychopath. There is a test for a psychopath, it can be taken online---50 questions. Psychopaths evidently refuse to take it. I don't know why that is.

I think it would be beneficial for a society to recognize a person who is a psychopath and make sure that they don't rise up to a position of power. The problem is that humans love a winner and will support a problem person as long as they feel like part of the winning team. But watch out. A psychopath will turn on a supporter so fast it will make his head spin, when he is no longer useful to them. Don't disagree with them.

I have wondered if the Middle-Age torch and pitchfork attacks on vampires were really about psychopaths, creatures that suck your "life's blood".

On the other hand, humans are a social species, one of the 6 or 7. We just eat, have fun, make babies. What's to stop us from overpopulating. Every docile species needs a predator species to keep them in check. Suppose that the psychopaths fulfill that function for humans? They certainly have a propensity for waging wars.

My Spirit Guides

I did come up with a list of my SGs, perhaps not complete.

1.	Shock	Elliot
2.	System Design	Albert
3.	Kinky Sex	Julie
4.	Art Appreciation	Carly
5.	Metaphysics	Harold
6.	Humiliation	Diane
7.	Humor	Larry
8.	Writing	Luther
9.	Body	Elise
10.	Tarot	Kathy
11.	Sailing	Jack

My Elliot

Elliot, the name I gave my SG who likes to shock people, exposes people to their deepest fears, a lot of times making them think about their own failings, imagined or not. Elliot can take over my voice without me knowing about it, until later, maybe. A lot of the time I don't even know it happened. It is seamless. As a result of this, I don't have many friends left. I don't like this behavior coming from me, but can't seem to control it, and he has always been with me, even as a kid, but now he is getting more accurate and virulent. I didn't realize what was going on until the last couple years.

I have been worried about doing an exorcism because I thought maybe Elliot was also my SG who aids me in computer system design, something I very much want to keep. But today I listed all of my "talents" and assigned a name to each SG who I assume is a specialist in those areas, and that process has made it clear that Elliot is probably separate from the others; if not, at least a separate function.

I did silently ask Elliot to not reveal other peoples' own fears to them unless they asked---like in a Tarot reading would be ok. And I believe that he agreed, since it hasn't happened since.

I also decided that figuring out which SG to address with a request was too much work, so I am going to just call out "Al" as a generic name for whichever SG is listening. Almon Brooks Wilder was my grandfather. He was pretty impressive, an advertising executive in Chicago who retired to a ranch in the Arkansas Ozarks, and finished up running a small town newspaper in Brooksville, FL.

EXPAND CONSCIOUSNESS

Why do we need another tenet? What is missing in the others?

What about "love", "purpose", "meaning"?

Worlds of Consciousness

There are 2 worlds of consciousness, the inside and the outside. Generally, we accept that the boundary is our skin. Our brains spend a lot of time taking care of the organs within our bodies, keeping them fed and healthy. That is the world of "separation", where we view other people and things as separate from ourselves.   Then there is the world of "union", where we see the connections between ourselves and everyone and everything, inside and outside of our bodies.

The world of union is pretty important because almost everyone pays attention to it in some way. Even the existentialists who don't believe that there is any externally derived meaning, have to deal with it, albeit in a negative way. That is what religion is all about, giving meaning to our lives. Whether we believe that what we worship is within or without doesn't matter so much. What we worship gives us a purpose, a moral compass of some form.

What is wrong with being an existentialist? Is it necessary to believe that there is something beyond ourselves? I personally don't think there is anything wrong with it. There is no proof that there is anything beyond, so why create a belief system which may not exist? Just deal with life as centered within and our decisions are all free-will. Actually, that *is* a belief system too.

As stated in the first tenet, "Reality IS". It is possible to go to higher consciousness, but it doesn't change reality, the physical. I see the search for "meaning" as the reason to spend time with a belief in the world of connections. Does it change anything? No, not in the physical. But what it does do is reveal the world of connections which can give us a sense of peace, even in tough times.

Sustainability

What percentage of our time can we spend in the world of union? That's where we have to be careful, because while in the higher consciousness, we can lose track of the world of separation which is necessary to continue to exist.

There are "masters" in India who live in higher consciousness most of the time. The one I heard about owns only a blanket, and travels around from town to town, sitting and sleeping under trees and does nothing toward survival. But when he talks, or just exists, others gain enlightenment through him, and consequently feed him and take care of his physical needs.

Think vs. Know

It seems that there are 2 types of knowledge from the world of separation and the world of union: "thinking" and "knowing". In astrology, the key mottoes for a Gemini are "I Think" and for an Aquarian, "I Know". I wondered what the difference was between "thinking" and "knowing". Then I realized that I already understood: "thinking" comes from logic, if some ideas are true, then this other idea must also be true---inference. While "knowing" is an idea that is experienced on a different deeper level and becomes more than an inferred result---it is a certainty, but without the logic to back it up.

Methods to Higher Consciousness

How to experience the world of union:

1.   Epiphany
2.   Meditation
3.   Near Death
4.   Sensory Deprivation
5.   Psychedelics
6.   Soul Gazing

Epiphany

An epiphany usually happens out of the clear blue sky. It isn't asked for, but arrives unannounced. I suppose it could be requested, and if your Spirit Guide (SG) agrees that the time is right, it could be delivered.

I have had several such moments this lifetime. I remember once driving down the highway into Jacksonville on the way to work. And there it was. Just a view of the sky ahead of me and the feeling that everything was right, a feeling of joy and peace. It didn't last long, but it was memorable.

For some people it is even stronger, with a definite message. Maybe the message is in the interpretation, because there are usually no words to go with it. We already know that words divide---just the act of categorizing a word divides this from that. While there are no words for the feeling of union, there is a knowing. Knowing what? Again, to answer that, words come into play and that's not what IT is.

"IT". A powerful word! Can you explain what "it" is? Existence? Alan Watts wrote an entire essay on the subject in a book entitled "This Is It". If you want to come closer to the understanding of the world of union, contemplate the word "it"---a meta-subject.

Many people have a religious experience for their epiphany. I don't have a problem with the experience, but I do object to their "realization" that they know what the one TRUE God or religion is. That is not the world of union---that is the world of separation.

Meditation

I personally have never entered the world of union during meditation, but I understand that some have. Meditation certainly helps to learn how to control the brain by stopping thinking. The brain is said to be "a useful tool, but a terrible master".

Going to higher consciousness involves passing through the lower levels where fear lies, so being able to control the brain is essential.

Near Death

There are many stories of people having out of the body experiences when they are near death, and or course, returning to tell us about it. They relate visions of tunnels of light, of meeting a dead relative, of angels, of peace and beauty. Many books have been written about those visions. I don't recommend doing it on purpose. Pretty risky.

Sensory Deprivation

It is possible to be catapulted into the world of union by shutting off all the senses. Floating in a pool of water with a mask on to omit light, smell, taste, and hearing allows the brain to explore possibilities without logic. Fasting can also work.

Psychedelics

LSD, psylocibin, mescaline---the 3 main chemicals which can take us out of the world of separation into the world of union. They can boost us through the levels of practical thinking into the world where there are no words. The "trips" usually last only a few hours and are safe, we always come back no matter how much we take.

Why is it called "tripping"? Because that is what it feels like---going somewhere foreign and then coming back---leaving what is familiar to pass through a region where the rules are different.

There are some evolutionists who theorize that the combinations of having opposable thumbs, walking upright, and ingesting magic mushrooms were what propelled our brains into what they are today. Although, it is also possible that animals spend most of their time in the world of union. We should ask them.

I once did ask a friend how to know when I am successfully tripping, having taken enough. He said I would know because I was "there". I love that. Another meta-word, "there". No words to describe it.

I have also tried to communicate with a tripping buddy what we were experiencing during the trip and the only thing we could both come up with was "Wow!"---not much of a description.

Soul Gazing

This is described in the book "The Spiritual Practices of Rumi" who was a Sufi mystic and poet. This book recommends the practice of staring into another's eyes for a long time in order for both to enter the world of union.

I have never tried this method---it sounds really deeply personal, almost scary.

But I have had some unusual experiences the last couple years. It isn't something I have desired or attempted, but comes on suddenly and surprisingly. It usually occurs when I am high on alcohol or marijuana. I can be looking at a friend and all of a sudden their face transformed into a gorgeous male or female face, still them, but different and more like a god or goddess. In the beginning I didn't know what I was seeing, but was so stunned by the appearance that I had to comment to them how beautiful they were. I think now that what I am seeing is the face of their soul. Evidently incarnating changes the perfect face into something not quite as perfect, probably for good reasons---most lives can be led more effectively without the face of a movie-star.

Another experience was had while hiking in the Catskills of New York with a friend. We had pitched our tent at the bottom of the trail for the night and got up early to begin the daylong hike over the spine of the hills. Before we started the ascent, we dropped a tab of acid. When we got to the top of the climb, we came across a man coming toward us on the trail with his dog. He reminded me of Ichabod Crane, skinny and gaunt. But what was really strange was that one side of his face was caved in dramatically, and even more strangely, his hound had the same disfigurement. I figured it was just the acid distorting my vision and behaved normally as we said hello and passed by. When we got aways away, I remarked to my friend that the man looked strange, and he replied that his face was caved in just like his dog. So evidently we both saw the same thing. We doubt that the man would have looked like that had we been straight, but we definitely saw something about the man's soul, or at least the incarnation. The other strange thing was that there were no dwellings up on that mountain and the closest other access to that trail was several hours along, so how did he get there coming toward us at that early hour---he didn't have a backpack.

Union

While in the world of union, there is a connection to something larger, an awe which inspires worship. There is the direct experience of being one with God or Allah, or in many religions, gods. There is always a human component also, the one who helps us, but has a direct connection to the god(s). That one is called Jesus or Mohammed or in many religions, ancestors. Of course, Wilderism would claim that they are actually Spirit Guides, but it doesn't matter.

We have the need to respect and revere something larger, and from that need, "worship" and "love" are born. It doesn't matter which god or gods or which intermediary being. We need to find something which is ultimately good somewhere, something larger than ourselves. And since people are constantly disappointing us, the thing to worship must be out there, or within, not to mention, "perfect", and also reflecting our love back to us.

Spending time with whatever belief system leads to a feeling of being connected to everything, to love everyone. On the other hand, those who follow the path to "hate", go more into the world of separation. "Separation/Union" are the two opposites directions in which a person can choose to go.

"Expanding Consciousness" is the path of union.

Native Americans

The Native Americans had their spirit guides and ancestors. I am not an expert on Indian religion or culture, but it seems to me that they worshipped at least the ancestors. They even had the nicest places set aside where the ancestors lived. These places were flowing with spiritual energy where they held rituals and went for retreats and had close contact with their spirit guides. And they worshipped those places so much that everyone knew that they were special and to be respected.

They had their "vision quests" where a young man would go out into nature alone and spend a few days looking for their SG and the "knowing" that accompanies it, and coming back changed.

The connection to nature is important---every animal embodies a human power or attribute, and studying the animals sheds light on human nature.

This in itself is an interesting study. How is it that each animal seems to emphasize a single human trait? It sounds like there is an overreaching intelligence somewhere in the creation of animals. This gets into the metaphysical 7 levels of consciousness where the top level is the Source Consciousness and the next level defines the characteristics of each type of entity.

There are many more indigenous cultures that share the ancestors worship.

Worship

So who or what can we worship?

There's God of course, or Allah, or Vishnu, or whoever---some entity so powerful that he/she is behind everything and everyone. I guess that perfection is not really required. It is about the power. God wants something to get done, it gets done. It's a *power* dimension. The weakest thing all the way up to the strongest.

Worship POWER!

Well, there's a need for it---some even claim that there is a section of the brain devoted to it.

And who can say it is wrong? What we worship is a belief-system. Not provable, but not unproven either.

Laws of Nature

I think for me it would be the laws of nature: physics, chemistry, biology. How it all works on the physical level. Now there is real power! And I am not talking about the power of those who know the rules, I am talking about the rules themselves.

How the rules all fit into each other, once understood. No contradictions, lots of extensions, but you don't find one physics rule which works sometimes and not other times, which sometimes has to give way for another rule which contradicts it, as long as we are talking about a "closed" system, in other words, where no external influences intervene.

And it is so interesting, the boundaries of the known. What is the meaning behind quantum mechanics? What is this dark matter stuff? Why is most of the universe made of dark matter and dark energy? So many questions, but also so much which has been discovered and proven and used, not to mention all that will be discovered.

Source of Rules

Then I ask, "where did these rules come from?" Don't know. I believe it is one of those things that is unknowable. Maybe. There are a lot of the numbers in physics and chemistry formulas, the formulas for what IS, those numbers being just the right value. A little less or a little more, and reality couldn't exist, at least not our universe. That brings up an interesting question. How is that the rules of physics are so finely tuned? The answer for some is "anthropomorphism", in other words, we are the creative beings and we created it, so of course it has to work. Others say that there are multiple universes and our existence is because we happen to be in one of the universes where life is possible. This gets into the "original" questions, which may never be answered. I mean even if you find out who or what has made the laws of nature, you never know if there isn't someone behind *them*, waiting to be discovered.

Religions

What to worship then? Pick your religion. I guess even science could be called a religion.

The real problem with religion is that there are interpreters who are no doubt inspired by Spirit Guides, imperfect beings with their own styles and viewpoints. The original idea is usually pure, but the morality which emanates from the interpreters is against nature sometimes---a lot of the time.

That's why I like science. The interpretation of any new theory has to be published, peer-reviewed, and capable of making predictions. It isn't either negative or positive, just what is, neutral. That's why it is so easy to not need a god with science, because there isn't a need for any "personality".

So what to worship? Comes down to: 1) you want it to be an intelligent entity, or 2) the laws of nature.

The second choice is interesting. It ignores the magical numbers in the laws which makes it possible to wonder where we come from. Don't know, yet. And that's ok. We keep learning more.

So that's it then. If you need a personality, you need an intelligence to worship. Doesn't seem wrong to me. What is it? Can't say. Most religions have personalities on top. That's what a specific religion is, the particular interpretation of this supreme entity, or entities. I guess you are born into it, or convert to it.

Science

That's why I like science. The rules of science work. There is no alternate interpretation---except for quantum mechanics, of course. But even without understanding the questionable cause of a rule, it can be used in practical ways. It's not idealistic, it is pragmatic. "I Don't know where it comes from, don't need to know, I just want to make use of it." The scientists' creed. Science versus religion.

Speaking of quantum mechanics, these are formulas which actually agree with physical measurements to incredible accuracy. There are also several interpretations about what the formulas mean, but no meaning has been found to be satisfactory, and certainly none of them is intuitive. A quantum physicist says it doesn't really matter---the formulas work even if we can't figure out why.

I agree with those who are into both science and religion. The science is known and respected and used, but the origination of the laws of nature can be questioned and explained too, and hopefully there is some entity to worship.

Morality

Does the morality of the science come in? Of course. Are you making people happy or aiding in the destruction of people? Most things that are created do both, in a sliding-scale, from the most loving to the most hating. And most peoples' morality is on another sliding-scale, from "denigrating it" to "worshipping it", with "don't care" somewhere in between. Poor Oppenheimer, the creator of the atomic bomb, what a dilemma between science and morality!

Soul Face

How about this? You could worship the person you are with. It's not new, but it does seem to be a logical choice.

View the person as an imperfect embodiment of a sacred being---the Soul to me. Try to see how the Soul decided to incarnate this time, the problems, the challenges, the successes.

Purpose

What is the purpose of the lifetime, or the period in the lifetime?

Could be learning, could be practicing, could be just experiencing---nothing to learn, just to experience having a body with all the adventures along the way. Could be working off karma.

Who's karma. If you are an incarnation only, then it must be the soul's karma. A Soul can have karma? The Soul is supposed to be the "accumulator of experience". Of course that is where karma would reside. It is believed that a "bad" human can delay the payment of their karma until the next lifetime. That indicates the Soul as being the maintainer of the karma, since that is where the incarnations come from.

Imagine discovering that the sole purpose of your existence is to work off a lot of your Soul's karma! We've got Scottish SGs on this one, the best slave masters! Isn't that the Story of Job?

Spiritual Experience

Let's change the subject now.

Let's talk about the spiritual experience itself, the mental state where the world of union is overlaid on the world of separation.

There are plenty of stories from those who have experienced near-death, of entering a world of love and warmness where harmony reigns. It changes them. They are no longer afraid of death. And they swear it was a real experience, not a brain hallucination.

I personally have experienced this world of connections many times using LSD. Used to do a bit, not a lot by some peoples' comparisons, and not much anymore. I could actually see the lines connecting things.

One of my favorite images during a trip was the feeling of rising above the clouds of my world of separation, actual clouds. And I felt like my head and shoulders were now above the clouds. And I looked out, and there I was, same head and shoulders, but a ways away, like different times and places. My feeling was "Ah, there I am during other trips", a good feeling.

I wonder if I could transmit lottery numbers to me in the past. Then I could be like the woman who played the same numbers for years, until she won big. She knew the right numbers, just not when.

Trips

I am certainly no expert on tripping, but I did do a bunch, maybe 50 my whole lifetime. Again that isn't many compared to some other people I have known. So all I can do is relate what my trips were like.

First of all, I am very cautious. I used to visit friends in a different city for a weekend and watch them trip, for at least a year. They didn't seem to go crazy or get sick, so eventually I agreed to join them. I remember sitting on the couch wondering what was going to happen, waiting, and then looking at my outstretched hand and seeing 10 fingers wavering on the one hand. It wasn't scary, but interesting. "Here I go", I thought.

A deeper trepidation for me was the fear of finding the "bottom" of my brain, to understand everything about my mind. It turns out that I discovered a depth that went on and on, way beyond what I could imagine. And not only mental, but physical as well---there was the feeling that my body extended beyond my skin and merged with the energies around me.

Coming on may take an hour, but it is a feeling of power for me. LSD produces a surging of my mind, an actual power buzz. And then things begin to dissolve, first my body, then my desires, and finally my mind. It could have been quite scary, but I knew enough to relax and just go with it.

This is why some people shouldn't do tripping. If they can't relax and just let go, the reaction can be dangerous to them because they may try to fix it---and that is the worst thing one can do while high. The "rule" is, while high, just observe and if you don't like something, make a mental note and try to fix it after the trip is over. That is an important rule which can save a lot of trouble. Experience with marijuana is important before tripping because it trains in the process of letting go---very different from alcohol.

I think it was a book by Timothy Leary I read. He was travelling with his dog and rented a room in a hotel in Paris, but he had to sneak the dog into his room because it wasn't allowed. While there, he dropped a tab of acid and waited for the trip to begin. But the dog indicated that it needed some outdoors. Tim knew he couldn't get the dog out and back while tripping, so decided to get the dog to go on a newspaper, which it did. Disposing of the poop was easy in the toilet, but what to do with the newspaper? If he put it in the trash it could be discovered, not least from its smell. His story in the book is much more interesting because he is explaining his whole thought process including the paranoias. Eventually he decided to just throw the paper out the back window, which he hated to do, but not much choice. And of course it fluttered open and became looped over a wire directly beneath his window, dirty side exposed. It is pretty funny, but the point is, don't try to fix anything while tripping.

To continue, getting "there" at the beginning of a trip involves the dissolution of everything. It seems that the body merges, so not so important anymore, then I couldn't remember my name, after that I lost my maleness, then my humanness, and became just pure thought energy. It is a glorious state of being, not alone, but a part of everything. It is hard to focus, difficult to do logic. When with someone else, both of us in this state, and I tried to communicate with them, words were totally inadequate. The only thing we could say was "Wow!".

Several trips I remember seeing my brain gone and thinking, "They are going to say that he used to be a programmer." A terrifying thought to me, but I just let it go and thought that if that is my future, so be it. Fortunately, I always got my programming skills back the next day.

What's also very interesting to me is that with my brain in such an unfocused state, I was still there analyzing what was going on with myself. Brain gone, but still watching. Who is that?

After another hour, the process of reconstruction begins, slowly. I get my logic back, then I become human, then male, then "Chris". And the next phase is really interesting. I start putting personality traits back on, one trait at a time. That's when I discovered that I could reject some traits, not needed anymore. That's why I called tripping "The Brain Vacuuming", clearing out useless junk and reintegrating the parts I needed or liked. It gave me the feeling that this process should be done on a regular basis, at least yearly, to clean out the garbage accumulated in my brain.

One of my good tripping buddies, we would sit on the grass and get beyond the "Wow" phase. One of the things LSD does is speed up the brain and remove the filters, to the point where I could see "idealets" forming and coming together into an idea which would eventually work its way out into a spoken sentence. It seemed to take minutes to say something, but actually it is in normal-time seen from the outside. Anyway, this friend and I would talk about a subject sparsely, then leap to the subject about the subject, and then do it again, getting more and more general with each "leap". For example, talking about the French language, then leaping to languages in general, and then the concepts of communication. We called it "metashifting" and we would love doing it with each other while tripping. That's where I got the name for my website, www.metashifting.com.

I tend to do that a lot, watching human behavior and realizing that it doesn't have to be like that---there are other possibilities for behavior. It is one of my failings---I laugh from delight when I see people behaving like a human so easily, and it upsets people because they think I am laughing at them. I laugh at the wrong times.

Then there are the "bad trips". My bad trips come from self-analysis, looking at my failings as a human. This happens to me on most trips, on the way back up, and it can last for hours during which I wish I could just fall asleep and be done with it. Usually the trip itself lasts 8 hours, and then another 4 before sleep. Again, my solution to these bad times is to just watch them and accept them and let them go.

Right after the first sleep comes the "loving stage". I wake up and appreciate all the people around me and want to tell them how great they are and how lucky I am to know them. This is not my normal behavior. This can last a few hours also.

One time in Florida I was living alone on my sailboat at a dock. My parents were working on their boat a couple of slips down. I was in the mood for a trip that evening and dropped a nice tab of acid I had. So to be further alone I went out into nature next to the marina, which was a bunch of tall weeds down by the water. Not a good setting, swampy, so I went back to the dock. Then I got the idea to sail my little Sunfish. I got into it and sailed out into the middle of the river. There wasn't much wind and the water was quite flat. The amazing thing I remember were the stars in the sky above me and their reflections in the water below me. It felt like I was in outer space completely surrounded by stars. It was wonderful!

After a while I decided to go back to my boat. I sailed to the dock, climbed up, and proceeded to tie the Sunfish to a piling, but I couldn't remember how to make a knot. I was still quite high. So I just wrapped the painter around the piling several times, which was sufficient for the night.

Passing by my parents' boat, I got the "brilliant" idea of inviting them to my boat for tea. They agreed to be over in a while, and I went down. I looked in the mirror and my face was changing colors and shapes. I thought that I had made a big mistake---how was I going to get through this while tripping my brain out without them knowing? I got the water on and the cups and tea bags out, but each thing I did was experienced as a gigantic project with beginnings, middles, ends---analysis, algorithms, dangers---brain going very fast.

I thought of another tripping rule, and that is that from the inside everything appears in slow motion, but from the outside, others see things I am doing in normal time.

They came aboard and were seated. I poured the tea and we began talking. This is where I first experienced watching "idealets" form. It would take me 15 minutes to formulate a simple answer to a question, and they didn't seem to notice. So I just played it straight. Years later I asked if they remembered that night, and did they notice anything strange. "Yes, and No".

After a couple years tripping just for fun or the novelty or the heaviness, I realized that it was deeper than that for me. Every trip I experienced something of eternity. So I decided that my new reason for tripping was to contact the universal consciousness. It always happened in some way, a realization of how connected I was with the universe. I found that to be very satisfying and rewarding.

Another rule: "set and setting". Mind "set" means getting to a mental/emotional state where I am peaceful. It is guaranteed that whatever is on my mind when I "come on", will be expanded and analyzed and made into the total reality, so I try to make it something happy and peaceful. "Setting" refers to the physical location for the trip, a place where negative events will not impinge---someplace with beauty and ease of use. I never know ahead of time exactly I am going to want during a trip, so I try to anticipate my wants and needs and set myself up with the best music (Pink Floyd, Grateful Dead, and some Van Morrison) and some easy to eat snacks and drinks.

Next I like to have 3 days set aside: the first to set things up and get into a peaceful happy state of mind, some meditation, second to do the trip itself which could take all day or all night depending, and third the come down with extra rest and sleep.

That brings up another aspect of tripping---that it is impossible to remember one state of consciousness when in another state. Events can be remembered, but not the state of consciousness. For example, when I am in pain from being sick, and then get well, I can't remember the pain. I can remember that I didn't like it and don't want to do it again, but not the actual pain itself. Same with getting high, even with marijuana---while high it is not possible to remember being straight, and vice versa.

I have learned to control the paranoia that goes with these drugs by thinking about what I would think if I was straight. I can't experience being straight, but I can logically figure out how my thinking would be if I was. And surprisingly, that usually works. It doesn't get rid of the paranoia, but turns it to an "out-there" instead of an "in-here". Paranoia is what turns a lot of people off about getting high.

Hope

Most religions are designed so that if you believe, you will be "saved". It may not be this lifetime, but later after death. This is important for those in misery, to believe in a "heaven" after death.

Humans have strong imaginations. I can imagine my own future. When the future is looking bleak, I can have "hope" that it will all work out alright.

What is the purpose of hope? To keep us going. Otherwise it would be easier sometimes to just give up and die. But one can always hope that it will get better.

I recently saw a temple in Bali where people were lined up to immerse their heads in a spigot with holy spring water. They had to dress up first, pray for awhile, then get in line. It was an involved procedure and then the water was cold. But it was supposed to be worth it because the "wish" made while getting splashed would surely come true. I wondered what all those people could be wishing for. Of course, it is the usual: money, love, power, enlightenment.

Then I wondered what the difference was between a "wish" and a "hope". My conclusion was that a "hope" was within your own belief system, totally possible, but a "wish" could be anything, no matter how unrealistic.

Wilderism says that a wish can come true, if it fits into your life plan, and your SG will make sure of that. Even if agreed to, it may not be immediately. But it is a partnership, so it doesn't hurt to ask.

Fate

The biggest question I have is this: how much of my life is fate and how much my own free-will? My belief-system is that the soul lives forever and needs to experience everything a human can experience. So, it incarnates humans into the world of time and space, thousands of them, all with different personalities and abilities, in different times and places. There is no "doing it to us", we are doing it to ourselves.

Therefore, there are events in each life that are decided on ahead of time. Those are what I would call "fate" or "destiny". In between those few major events, there is a lot of life which can be led using free-will. What can be achieved during the non-fate times is style. Our lives are a canvas on which we paint our existence, utilizing our powers to develop a picture of what? Beauty? Power? Love?

Visualizing a life, we could say that the fate-events are like mountain peaks, not open for modification. But in between are all these valleys and hills where we have the free-will to design our own lives. But underneath that, there is the need to setup the fate-events.

This is where I believe that Spirit-Guides come in. They help with all aspects of our lives. We have some SG which are assigned to us for the entire life and other specialists that come in just when needed. Since they know our future, they can shepherd us gently to get the abilities which will be needed later on.

But if we don't like the way things are going, we can modify our lives and our SGs will help with that also. Of course, they have their own proclivities and styles. I think of it as a cooperation, my own free-will and style matched with my SGs' styles and their knowledge of the coming fate-events. In other words, there are some things I can change and some I can't.

The trick is knowing the difference. I like to think of events in terms of quantum mechanics, where the Schrodinger wave equation stretches to infinity very flat, but has peaks and valleys before and after the main event. There are hills before the big event that can indicate what is coming, and these can be seen if I am watching for them. But again, sometimes I don't like the direction the hills are indicating. So, I try my free-will, asking my SGs to help me modify the future, and if that works, great. But other times, it doesn't work. That's "fate". In that case I just have to "go with it", like while tripping. Not much choice anyway. Maybe my SGs and I can add some style to the event.

Don't forget that it is not just about us. What we do impacts other peoples' lives also, some directly and some just by hearsay. Thinking about that, it gets very complicated---begins to look magical. But it is just the world of union which we don't normally see. Those may be some of the "hills" in our lives, the ones necessary to get someone else where they are going.

To me, thinking about my life like that gives it "meaning". Will it "save" me? Maybe not. But it does give me the belief that it all isn't just pointless, which makes it easier to handle the negative fate events.

Of course, there are the positive fate-events also. I try not to avoid them.

Spirit Guide Times

I have recently come to the conclusion that a lot of the urges which our SGs give us, are designed so that we do what the SG knows we will do in the future.

I like the Woody Allen movie "Midnight in Paris". Our hero, Gil, goes to the past and meets many famous people, one of whom is Luis Bunuel. He is famous for the film, which doesn't exist at the time, "The Exterminating Angel" about a dinner party where no one can leave. Gil tells him that he should consider writing a movie about a dinner party where no one can leave. Luis asks, "Why can't they leave?" Answer: "They just can't". In the Woody Allen movie, it didn't make sense to Luis at the time, but later on he did write "The Exterminating Angel".

Paul McCartney claimed that his songs came from his dreams. In his movie, "Get Back", about the Beatles developing the songs, he starts with a vague notion of the song and then you can hear them enhance it into the great music we know, it evolves over the space of hours or days. As the creator of that song, he knows somehow what is right and what is wrong, and with the aid of his partners, makes it happen. Did his SG know the final product and urge its creation and then supply the "rights and wrongs"?

Do SGs only urge creations which are notable? Or is every major event in a person's life, somehow important? What about negative events like a murder? Urged? Or a mistake?

An interesting philosophical question. It is described beautifully in a scene in the movie "The Witches of Eastwick". As Daryl, the devil, is being attacked by the witches, he asks the church congregation, "God isn't perfect, everybody makes mistakes. But women! Did God do it to us on purpose? Or is it a mistake? Because if it is a mistake, maybe we can invent a vaccine."

I am sure women have the same thoughts about men.